Absolute Crime Presents:

School Massacre

15 Horrifying School Shootings That Shook the Nation

By William Webb

Absolute Crime Books

www.absolutecrime.com

Cover Image © VIPDesign - Fotolia.com

Table of Contents

About Us

Absolute Crime publishes only the best true crime literature. Our focus is on the crimes that you've probably never heard of, but you are fascinated to read more about. With each engaging and gripping story, we try to let readers relive moments in history that some people have tried to forget.

Remember, our books are not meant for the faint at heart. We don't hold back — if a crime is bloody, we let the words splatter across the page so you can experience the crime in the most horrifying way!

If you enjoy this book, please visit our homepage to see other books we offer; if you have any feedback, we'd love to hear from you!

Introduction

Aside from homes, schools are thought to be the second safest haven for children. But what if the institution that is designed to nurture and educate our children suddenly becomes the location for some of most horrific events we can imagine?

School shootings have grown more rampant over the years, a condition that has become a serious crisis. Violence has become a part of our everyday lives and sadly, we all have slowly become accustom to seeing the reports on the news.

Apart from setting safety measures in place to prevent these crimes from happening, it is important to gain a better understanding of what caused these teenagers to plot these plans and commit unthinkable evils.

Let's take a look at some of the most horrific school shootings in history.

Erfurt Massacre

It was on April 26, 2002 that the Germans were issued a horrific wakeup call by a 19 year old boy named Robert Steinhäuser.

It was supposed to be an ordinary Friday for the students of the Johannes Gutenberg School in the bustling city of Erfurt. By some cruel twist of fate, the students witnessed firsthand how the security of the school was breached and how the once quiet corridors reverberated with gunshots.

It was on this day that the former student Steinhäuser stormed into the classrooms and killed a total of 13 teachers and 2 students, along with a secretary and a policeman who responded and arrived early on the scene.

While he was reloading his gun, Steinhäuser suffered a temporary psychic collapse. Seeing it as an opportunity to put a stop to the killing spree, a history and art teacher managed to summon up the courage to shove Steinhäuser into a nearby room and lock him up. With nowhere to go, Steinhäuser shot himself.

Police on the scene identified the weapon used by Steinhäuser as a Glock 17 9mm pistol, which is capable of firing 17 shots from a single magazine. Steinhäuser also carried with him a 20-gauge shotgun but he was not able to use it. According to reports, he fired a total of 40 shots from the pistol but he carried over 500 more rounds of reserve ammunition, which was found in a black bag that he left near the spot where he shot himself.

Apparently, the massacre was not a spur of a moment thing as evidence showed he was well prepared. The bloodbath at the school was considered to be one of the worst shootings that has rocked Germany since World War II.

An American Condition

High school rampages were believed to be an "American condition" and were not considered a problem that plagued Germany. In the investigation following the event, the massacre may have been retribution of sorts, as it was found out that Steinhäuser was previously expelled by the school for forgery of a medical excuse.

Different sectors of society raised alarm at the disturbing turn of events, claiming the "American problem", where violence seems to be a part of daily living, has reached their country.

According to Steinhäuser's mother, hours before the rampage, her son claimed he was going to school in order to take a Math exam. She even shared that as he was leaving the house, she wished him good luck. She was not aware that the teenager was expelled two months prior to the incident but did not tell his parents about it. In fact, both the mother and father were led to believe their child went to school every day and was working hard to get his high school diploma.

A little before 11AM, Steinhäuser managed to enter the school building and headed straight to the restroom where he quickly changed into an all-black ninja outfit and a ski mask. He went straight to the classroom where his former classmates were taking the Math exam.

An account from witnesses revealed that as Steinhäuser charged into the classroom, he announced he was not going to write anything before he started firing. As the students ran out of the room, Steinhäuser came after them. One teacher was seen tapping her index finger on her forehead, a silent language that signaled he was insane. In retaliation, Steinhäuser pointed a gun at her head and pulled the trigger.

According to the students who managed to escape his wrath, it seemed as if Steinhäuser was intent on searching out the teachers and killing them on sight with point blank shots, aiming right at their heads. In a matter of minutes, dead bodies started piling up along the school corridors.

It was clear that Steinhäuser managed to kill everyone he aimed at, mostly headshots which showed he was a trained marksman. Aside from the teachers, Steinhäuser also shot down a 15-year-old boy and a 14-year-old girl, who were hit through a closed door. Authorities surmise Steinhäuser had no intention of killing students and the two were merely killed by accident. This is in consideration of the fact that all of the other victims were hunted down with precision.

One victim, a teacher, was seen running towards her car but in her haste, she tripped. Steinhäuser shot her in the leg, and then as he got near her, he shot her three times in the head. It was the school janitor who called for help. When the police finally arrived, Steinhäuser confronted the arriving officer and exchanged fire with him. He

managed to kill one policewomen before he fled to the
rear part of the building.

The Accidental Hero

It was Reiner Heise, a 60-year-old history and art teacher,
who put an end to the bloodbath. According to him, he
encountered Steinhäuser when he opened a door looking
for students. Instead of finding the students, he saw the
end of the rampager's gun, which was pointed at his chest.

For some unknown reason, at that same moment
Steinhäuser decided to take off his ski mask in front of the
teacher. When Heise recognized the student, he started to
talk to Steinhäuser, challenging him to pull the trigger but
to look at the teacher in the eyes if he should shoot him.

However, instead of taking up the dare, Steinhäuser
replied that it was enough killings for the day. The
teacher, upon recognizing the possible change of heart,
motioned his former student to an empty classroom,
inviting him to talk. At this time, Steinhäuser had slowly
let down his guard, which the teacher took advantage of
by shoving Steinhäuser into the room and locking him
inside, then Heise ran to the principal's office.

In hindsight, Heise shared he did not have time to be
afraid, and perhaps unlike the other teachers who were
brutally murdered, Steinhäuser may have liked him and
did not consider him an enemy.

The police then swarmed the building in an effort to close
in on Steinhäuser. Instead of engaging the authorities in

another gunfight, Steinhäuser chose to commit suicide by shooting himself in the head.

The Aftermath

Hours after the rampage, police found out that Steinhäuser owned a personal website, which was recently updated. Initially, the police thought Steinhäuser may have had an accomplice but later dismissed the idea and concluded that hackers had done the changes on the site as a prank.

The night after the rampage, all church bells across Erfurt rang in mourning and the cathedrals were filled with mourners who wept inconsolably. The school also called in a psychiatrist to help the students in coping with the horror of the massacre. Everyone seemed to have the same question in their minds: *"Why?"*

For the next three days following the incident, the school was sealed off as the police conducted a more thorough search for clues in their efforts to piece together the horrific chain of events. Classes were also cancelled for a week to give the students adequate time to mourn for the death of their schoolmates and teachers.

All evidence suggests that the massacre was an act of revenge by Steinhäuser, against the system and the teachers who he felt failed him. It was found that the trouble started when Steinhäuser failed an exam called the Abitur, which is the equivalent of the SAT in the United States or Britain's A-Levels. Upon failing the rigorous examination, Steinhäuser was forced to repeat his final year in high school.

The exam is said to be critical, as all students are required to pass it before they can enter college. Without it, the student will also be blocked from ever getting a decent job or an opportunity to further his or her education. When Steinhäuser was expelled from school for forging his medical excuse, he apparently lost the opportunity of taking the Abitur exam ever again.

Jokela School Shooting

School shootings are often considered to have an American origin. But while it may be more common in the United States, every so often, we are all reminded that it can happen anywhere and at any time. It's an unexpected catastrophe that no one will ever get used to.

In Finland, the Jokela school shooting was a tragedy that is claimed to be an isolated case but sadly, it is not the first homicide that took place at a Finnish school. But while such tragedies rarely occur, its impact on society can be dramatic, especially on the perceived safety schools provide their students.

In order to understand school shootings in general, it should be taken into account in its broader social and cultural context.

Days Leading Up To the Incident

Jokela is one of the major municipal centers of Tuusula. The school is located in the central district of Jokela. In the days leading up to November 7, 2007, the investigation showed that Pekka-Eric Auvinen had carefully planned and prepared for the massacre, even as early as March 2007.

Authorities were able to locate Auvinen's diary where he had written about his plan to initiate an operation against the human race. He had also written about his plans to wreak havoc and mayhem around him. He had vividly described his plans of being armed and ready for his special operation by autumn. At 18 years old, Auvinen had already come to terms with the fact that he would likely die in carrying out his plan.

In Auvinen's diary, he also shared his thoughts about how he wished his act would be something people would remember forever and he hoped it would leave a lasting impact on the world. He also expected many people would follow in his footsteps and like him; they too share the fascination and admiration of how school killings were carried out across the globe.

In fact, reflected in the entry of his diary dated April 20, 2007, he celebrated the Columbine school killings anniversary and even shared his disappointment of how the killer's propane bomb had failed to explode.

By May 2007, Auvinen had started writing his manifesto 'Natural Selector,' which was entitled 'How Did Natural Selection Turn Into An Idiocratic Selection?' This document was uploaded to his website on November 5, 2007 in both Finnish and English versions. According to the reports, he was still doing the finishing touches to the manifesto the night before the shooting.

Sometime in August, it was reported that Auvinen had visited the shooting range and had a chance to shoot with a real weapon. When October rolled around, he was able to acquire a firearms permit and immediately used it to buy ammunition and a gun at a local gun shop.

On November 5, 2007, Auvinen went into the woods and practiced his shooting skills. This was evident based on the date he uploaded the video online. Additionally, during the last few days leading up to the rampage, he was an active participant on an internet forum about the Columbine school killings. In fact, he had published a photo of himself holding a gun and a video montage of the video surveillance camera materials he had compiled from the Columbine school killings.

Authorities were able to trace Auvinen having engaged in private discussions with another community member a couple of nights before the incident. In their exchanges, he had implied his plan to go to a school with his gun. However, when he was asked for more details, Auvinen refused to provide answers.

On the night before the killings, Auvinen had spent time creating and editing a number of text files, which included a series of farewell messages to his family. He made it clear in his messages that he was committing the crime in an effort to help make the society a better place. He also claimed that if things had been better, the killings would be unnecessary.

The Rampage

On the 7th of November, the day of the incident, Auvinen did not attend his first lesson but instead chose to spend his time surfing online. At 9:33 AM, he uploaded a video on YouTube, which showed the school center and a reddish image of Auvinen pointing his gun at the camera. Rock music was playing loudly in the background.

By 11AM, he edited the video and sent out messages to an online forum community about school killings, cryptically stating history would be made that day. The day he had chosen to carry out his evil deed happened to be the 70th anniversary of the October Revolution.

At 11:28AM, Auvinen switched off his computer and rode his bicycle to school. Instead of going in through the usual entrance, he parked at the corner of a pond closest to the school building. He then entered through the basement, which was just below the school canteen.

At that time, classes were well underway for the lower levels while secondary school students were already having their lunch.

Auvinen made his first shot when he encountered a secondary school student. He then went to the ground floor lavatories. Students had started to notice the unnamed student slumped face down on the floor, who they initially thought had a concussion. And while many students testified that they heard the shots, they failed to entertain the idea that they were gunshots.

Standing at the doorway of the lavatory, Auvinen again took out his gun to kill in cold blood. This time he shot two students in rapid succession. At the time, some students had recognized Auvinen. He then shot another student when he noticed she was trying to escape through a corridor. Within the first four minutes of the first shot, he was able to kill six people.

The head teacher made an announcement using the school's PA system instructing students to stay in their respective classrooms. Upon hearing this, Auvinen fired successive shots, totaling 53 cartridges, based on the investigation conducted. He was also heard shouting, *"I will kill all of you!"*

Auvinen then decided to go two stories up. He aimed at students who were lounging on a bench. However, the first one managed to escape, while the other was fatally wounded. He then decided to move towards the first floor just in front of the school canteen, shooting through the locked glass doors.

Students hurriedly left the canteen by escaping through the kitchen door. Auvinen shot another five rounds inside the canteen and when he saw the education welfare teacher trying to flee the scene, he went after the teacher and shot him in the head, his eighth victim.

Auvinen then took position near the school's main entrance and fired two shots at the police officers who had responded. Instead of fighting it out with the authorities, Auvinen retreated to a lavatory next to the canteen. Seeing he had no other way out, Auvinen shot himself in the head. He was the ninth casualty.

Based on the cartridge casings found at the scene, police reported Auvinen fired a total of 75 shots inside the school. However, there were also 328 bullets unused and 250 more found in his bag.

Elimination

Unlike other school shootings that were mostly spurred by revenge or anger, Auvinen's motives were to eliminate those he deemed unfit to live. He had even called himself the 'social Darwinist'.

Aside from the YouTube video, Auvinen had also posted a manifesto on another website claiming that killing and death should not be considered a tragedy since not all human lives are worth saving or important.

He also made it clear that he was acting of his own volition and claimed that it was his war, a war against humanity, the government and the general masses whom he considered weak-minded. He had also posted online that there is no God and there is no real purpose for man's existence.

Winnenden School Shooting

On March 11, 2009, a secondary school operated in the southwestern part of Germany had witnessed a gruesome series of killings, perpetrated by one of its former students. This incident by far produced one of the highest number of deaths, with a total of 16 people who were randomly executed.

The person behind this tragedy was a 17-year-old boy named Tim Kretschmer, who had already graduated from the school the previous year before the incident occurred. Aside from the dead bodies, there were also several people injured.

Massacre in Broad Daylight

Kretschmer entered his former school in Albertville at around 9:30 AM where he unceremoniously opened fire using a 9mm Beretta, a semi-automatic pistol. According to several accounts of eyewitnesses, Kretschmer went up to the first storey of the building and made a beeline for the chemistry laboratory and two classrooms located on the floor.

In the two classrooms, Kretschmer managed to kill 7 students along with one female teacher. According to police reports, all his victims were shot in the head. In response to the attack, the school principal used the PA system to alert the other teachers of the situation through a coded announcement. This allowed the teachers to respond promptly and lock their classroom doors.

The local police responded to the scene following an emergency call from a student, which was made at around 9:33 AM. Three police officers arrived on the scene two minutes later and entered the school premises in the hopes of putting a halt to the shooting. Instead of surrendering, Kretschmer shot at them before fleeing the building, killing two female teachers along the way. In the school alone, the authorities reported that Kretschmer fired a total of 60 rounds.

The Escape and Carjacking

At the sight of the police, Kretschmer decided to flee the scene. On his way, he also murdered a 56-year-old gardener tending the park of the psychiatric institution nearby. By this time, a large number of armed police officers were already on the scene and had worked on securing the school building. Others focused on searching for the gunman for several hours but with no success.

At around 10:00 AM, Kretschmer had managed to hijack a Volkswagen Sharan minivan, which was parked in Winnenden. He took to the rear seat and at gunpoint, he ordered the driver to drive towards Wendlingen, which was approximately 40 kilometers from Winnenden. This journey took them to the western part of the city, traveling through several towns and districts before they drove through the B14 dual carriageway, which was through the Heslach Tunnel. At the Wendlinger junction, the hostage and driver steered towards the grass verge and managed to jump from the vehicle, running towards a police patrol car. This all occurred around 12 noon.

A Shootout in Wendlingen

After the driver escaped, Kretschmer also left the car then ran towards an industrial area nearby. He then entered a Volkswagen car showroom at the main entrance. He threatened a salesperson on sight and demanded a key for one of the vehicles. However, the salesperson managed to escape while Kretschmer was distracted.

In retaliation, the gunman fired and murdered another salesperson along with one customer, firing a total of 13 bullets into the bodies of the victims. While he reloaded his gun, another salesperson and a visitor managed to flee through the rear exit of the car showroom.

The gunman walked out of the building and shot at a passing vehicle; however, the driver was able to escape without injury. By this time, more police officers arrived on the scene and a shootout ensued. One police officer was able to hit Kretschmer on each leg.

With an injury, Kretschmer returned to the showroom and shot at the police who were moving in to surround the building. Kretschmer exited using the rear door and ran across the yard where he shot at and managed to injure two police officers who were riding in an unmarked police car.

Kretschmer continued to fire at random, shooting people and buildings along the way. According to some eyewitnesses, the 17-year-old boy reloaded his gun before he shot himself in the head, ending his life. The last few seconds of the shootout with the police was captured on video with a mobile phone camera. According to forensic reports, Kretschmer had fired a total of 112 rounds all throughout the shooting spree.

The Psychology of a Teen Killer

Kretschmer was a resident of Leutenbach, a neighboring municipality. The previous year before the incident, he graduated from Albertville Realschule with relatively low grades. His poor performance and failing grades in middle school prevented him from being granted an apprenticeship in preparation for a career in commerce. According to his former classmates and friends, Kretschmer was a frustrated and lonely person who often felt he was rejected by society in general.

However, Kretschmer was known to be an avid tennis player and even had hopes of playing professionally. According to one Croatian table tennis player named Marko Habijanec who coached Kretschmer, he remembered the boy as someone who was a bit spoiled and his mother was always there, eager to fulfill his every wish.

Habijanec also shared that Kretschmer always had a problem with accepting defeat. He remembered that as a boy, Kretschmer always displayed quite a temper, often throwing his racket and yelling. Kretschmer also happened to have a high opinion of his tennis skills, but was often openly scorned and belittled by his teammates.

According to media reports, Kretschmer was known to enjoy video games like *Counter Strike*. In fact, a day before the killing spree, he even played a video game called *Far Cry 2* online. He also played with airsoft guns, which he had used for shooting in the forest behind his home and in the privacy of his basement.

The police investigated his personal computer and found that Kretschmer apparently had a secret fascination with sadomasochistic scenes where men were bound and humiliated by women.

Based on police records, Kretschmer did not have any criminal records prior to the incident. However, according to press reports, he allegedly received treatments at the Weissenhoff Psychiatric Clinic as an in-patient. Upon his discharge, he was supposed to continue his medical treatment as an outpatient but failed to do so.

According to the police report, Kretschmer was suffering a form of clinical depression although his family had denied such claims and firmly maintained that their son never received any psychiatric treatment. This was in clear contrast to the report furnished to the prosecutor's office where it was stated Kretschmer had met with a therapist five times. Their sessions mainly covered his violent urges and growing anger. This delicate piece of information was said to have been relayed to the parents.

A few weeks following the incident, the police were able to uncover videos on the internet, which showed Kretschmer announcing his plans a few hours before the incident. The teenager had also taken the time to write a letter addressed to his parents stating he was suffering and he could not go on.

Germany mourned for this truly heart-breaking event, which led to parents and the general public to question the safety schools afforded to students as well as why these teenagers were given access to ammunition by their parents in the first place. Many of the victims were teenagers, whose lives were inadvertently cut short due to the senseless killings.

It was later found out that Kretschmer got his ammunition from his father, who was allegedly a member of a local marksmanship club. While the father had several guns in safekeeping, all placed inside the gun safe, it was the Beretta that was left unsecured.

Toulouse and Montauban Shootings

Since time immemorial, religion has been a cause of major dissension among people. In the case of the Toulouse and Montauban shootings, the perpetrator Mohammed Merah killed his victims simply because they were Jews.

The Man Who Pulled the Trigger

Merah was a 23-year-old French citizen of Algerian descent. He was also a self-styled al Qaeda jihadist, as authorities found out, who was responsible for killing seven people. Merah was not an immigrant but was born in a suburb in Toulouse and one of the 7 million French-born Muslims in the country.

Merah grew up as a juvenile delinquent even as a young boy. By the time he was in his teens, he had managed to accumulate 15 acts of violence. While this may be appalling to some, this was not something new in the neighborhood he grew up.

His first arrest involved theft in 2005 and he was subsequently arrested for a series of criminal offenses in 2005, 2007 and 2009. In 2011, Merah reportedly went to Pakistan and stayed there for about two months. According to reports, the domestic intelligence agency of France DCRI had reports about his trip and he was even suspected of being involved in a radical Islamic movement.

A Series of Attacks

The attacks that took the lives of seven innocent people was part of a series of three separate shootings that took place in March of 2012 in Toulouse as well as in Montauban, which is just about 45 kilometers away. The victims included one teacher, three children and three soldiers who were shot down between the 11th and the 19th of March.

Each shooting was carried out in broad daylight by a single gunman that was aboard a scooter, and in the first two shootings soldiers were specifically targeted as victims. However, the third shooting took place at a local Jewish school, killing the children along with one teacher.

Days before the killings, a Yamaha T-Max 500cc scooter was reported stolen in the Toulouse area. Apparently, Merah had contacted a dealership within the Toulouse area to seek advice on how to take out the GPS tracking device of a scooter. The dealership owner Christian

Dellacherie suspected that this was the man behind the stolen vehicle and notified the police.

Another clue that led to the identity of the gunman was the email account that was used to communicate with the first victim. On March 11, Sunday, Imad Ibn-Ziaten, who was a 30-year-old staff sergeant of the 1st Airborne Transportation Regiment was shot dead, just behind Chateau de l'Hers school.

In the investigation, authorities found that Sgt Ibn-Ziaten had previously posted an ad online selling a Suzuki Bandit motorcycle. Merah had arranged a meeting with him by getting in touch through email. In the investigation, it was learned that Sgt Ibn-Ziaten received a call on his mobile phone minutes before the attack.

A Trail Of Dead Bodies

Sgt Ibn-Ziaten was shot in the head and his motorcycle was left beside him. When the French police traced the communication, the email account was used by Merah's family.

The second shooting involved three soldiers. Two were members of the Airborne Combat Engineering Regiment 17th Division: Private Mohamed Legouad, 26 and Corporal Abel Chennouf, 24, were both killed. Like Sgt Ibn-Ziaten, the two were reported to be of North African origin.

The third soldier was a paratrooper named Corporal Loic Liber, 28 who was from the French overseas region of the Guadeloupe. However, he was lucky enough not to be killed but was left in a comatose state.

Since Merah chose to take down his victims in broad daylight, there were a number of eyewitnesses to the Montauban attack, which occurred just outside a shopping center. According to reports, before he opened fire, Merah moved aside an old lady who was standing in the line of fire.

People described the gunman to be exceptionally calm and had even stopped to change the pistol's magazine.

The fourth victim was a seven-year-old girl named Myriam Monsonego, who was the daughter of a head teacher. According to reports, the girl was grabbed by the hair before she was shot in the head. He also killed Rabbi Jonathan Sandler along with his two sons.

Compared to the previous attacks, the third attack seemed to be different as the gunman was firing indiscriminately, shooting people inside the school grounds without any clear target. It seemed like Merah shot at anyone he could see, not particular whether he killed adults or children. He was even seen chasing children into the school. To conceal his identity, Merah wore a motorcycle helmet with the visor down. It was later found that all throughout the attacks, Merah was wearing a GoPro camera to document his killing prowess.

In all three shootings, the same Colt 45 pistol was used, which was said to be the same gun thrown during the siege at Merah's apartment on the 21st of March.

Encounter with the Police

Following the lead on the email address used to communicate with his first victim, the French police were able to track down Merah in his apartment. He had apparently detected the authorities were in the area and he fired a shot when one officer knocked on the door of his apartment. The police were able to communicate with Merah and informed him of their intention to keep the entire building under siege, which lasted for 32 hours, which was one of the longest in the history of France.

Eventually, a raid team was sent in and engaged in a firefight with Merah, who was hiding out in the bathroom. Merah attempted to escape by jumping out of the window while still firing shots. However, a sharpshooter fired a single fatal shot through Merah's head, killing him on the spot.

According to police reports following the shootout, Merah was armed with an Uzi machine gun, Kalashnikov assault rifle and several handguns. Police also found out that Merah had petrol and other key ingredients for making makeshift bombs.

Based on the report, a Special Forces expert shared that he had never seen any suspect resist arrest with such ferocity. During the siege, Merah first declared that he would be willing to negotiate only to recant his statement and asserted he planned to resist arrest and even stated he was prepared to use lethal force if the need arose. Merah even told the authorities that he planned to *die as a mujahedeen*.

Aftermath

The tragedy gripped the hearts of many in France and Merah's crimes were considered to be an act of terrorism.

However, the counterterrorism chief denied that their force had failed to pick up on a serious threat and they had not taken a report on Merah.

Once again, the nation was shown that most people are divided and some go to war due to their beliefs. In an effort to diffuse the tension and discourage closer public scrutiny, statements issued by the French government and its police were designed to deflect issues surrounding religion and the Muslim versus Jew war.

Merah had claimed that he was a *jihadist* and that he was operating under al Qaeda. According to the official reports, Merah committed the killings in his efforts to avenge all the Palestinian children and to also take revenge on the government and army of France because of their foreign interventions.

Merah's attacks were recognized as acts of terrorism. Based on further investigation, the authorities believed that he acted on his own and had planned to carry out more attacks, particularly on soldiers and police officers. In fact, Merah's only regret was that he was not able to kill more people. He had openly boasted that he believed he had brought "France to its knees" with his attacks.

In addition, investigations revealed that Merah had not intended to carry out a suicide mission and had every intention to stay alive. However, the siege and his ferocious efforts to engage the authorities in a gunfight brought an end to his life.

2014 Moscow School Shooting

School shootings are no longer considered to be only an American problem as it has been clearly shown such a tragedy can happen anywhere. Sadly, despite the numerous horror stories of lives lost in previous shootings, no one can fully prepare for its occurrence and apparently, it is not something that can be always prevented from happening.

The School Rampage

On February 3, 2014 at around 11:40 AM, a 10th grade student named Sergei Gordeyev entered his school, along the Otradnoye District in Moscow, armed with a small caliber rifle and a hunting carbine. According to reports, Gordeyev was able to evade the school's security because there were turnstiles, which had been recently replaced. Nevertheless, a security guard was able to stop the teenager upon seeing he was carrying ammunition.

In response, Gordeyev cocked his rifle and demanded the security guard lead him to the biology classroom. Since under the Russian law security guards are generally not allowed to carry any firearms, all he could do was press a panic button in order to alert the police before he followed Gordeyev's instructions.

When Gordeyev reached the classroom, he immediately fired at a 30-year-old biology and geography teacher named Andrey Kirillov. He initially fired and hit the teacher's stomach. Gordeyev then approached the teacher and simply asked him if he was still alive. When the teacher replied yes, Gordeyev then placed a second bullet in his head, killing the teacher instantly.

After this, Gordeyev turned to the 10th grade students in the classroom and held them hostage. At this time, the police had already arrived at the scene. Upon seeing this, Gordeyev started firing at them from the classroom's window. Gordeyev was able to kill a 38-year-old police officer and also managed to injure his partner.

Reinforcement police squads then arrived at the school, including a helicopter that landed in the school's yard. The authorities had also invited Gordeyev's father who was asked to wear a bulletproof vest and entered the school in order to assist in the negotiation with his son.

During the talk with his father, Gordeyev eventually agreed to release the students and was then apprehended by the police. Luckily, no students were injured or killed in the incident.

The Motive

Unlike other school shootings that typically had many complex reasons, with students plotting massacres to purge society or something to that effect, this particular case was a result of simple anger. According to the speculations of other students, the shooting was most likely a result of a personal conflict between Gordeyev and the biology teacher that spiraled out of control, leading the teenager to kill the teacher.

Apparently, Gordeyev was a straight A student who was hoping to graduate with distinction. According to his classmates, Gordeyev worked hard to achieve good grades and sometimes even resorted to memorizing the textbook, or some of its relevant pages. It was said that the biology teacher did not approve of this and refused to give Gordeyev an A despite his efforts. This jeopardized Gordeyev's plans of graduating with honors. Gordeyev and Kirillov were said to have known each other some years ago. This is because Kirillov used to be the former master of Gordeyev's class.

Gordeyev's Background

Gordeyev was from a family that served in the military. Both his grandfather and his father were members of the armed forces. In addition, the weapons that were used during the school shooting were property of his father who was serving in the Federal Security Service and was also a hunting enthusiast.

According to the father, the rifles were safely locked inside a safe at the family's home. However, the teenage boy knew the combination. Upon investigation conducted by the authorities, Gordeyev had an account in one of the Russian social networking platforms wherein it featured only a single video clip, that of the fastest shooter in the world.

Aside from Gordeyev's keen interest in firearms, he was also attending classes in combat sambo, which is a popular form of Russian martial arts. However, one of his classmates shared that Gordeyev always struggled to fit in. For instance, when he cracked a joke, nobody in the room would laugh. He was not immune to feeling like an outcast. Gordeyev saw and felt it, and had started to feel bad about it.

According to authorities, it was clear that the school shooting was not a spur of the moment decision. In the investigation, it was revealed that Gordeyev fired 11 shots at the police officers who first responded to the alarm, managing to kill one and injure another. This incident had come amid the strengthened security across Russia as it prepared for the Winter Olympics that was held in Sochi.

Gordeyev was placed in the custody of the police and would be consequently charged with hostage taking, homicide and endangering the life of a police officer. Gordeyev was facing 12 to 20 years in prison for the crimes he committed. However, during the trial there was an order for a battery of psychological tests to be carried out. This would help to fully determine the triggers that pushed an exceptionally smart student to start what is known to be an unprecedented school shooting in Moscow.

The trial of Gordeyev is pending the outcome of the psychological tests and due to start again in August of 2014.

The Aftermath

While Russia is certainly not a stranger to violence, incidents of school shootings are extremely rare. However, in recent history, Russian schools are among some of the most gruesome attacks going back to September 2004. In the incident, 34 insurgents of the nationalist-Islamist group managed to take 1,100 hostages inside an elementary school during its first day of classes in North Ossetia.

In the Gordeyev case, authorities and citizens heaved a collective sigh of relief upon knowing it was not an act of terrorism. Nevertheless, the incident warranted a full investigation and understanding as to the factors that triggered the attack especially from a straight A student. In addition, the incident also called for a full review of the security guidelines of the school and how to ensure the safety of students.

The school shooting had managed to unnerve the entire nation and had somehow contributed to the extreme sense of unease and paranoia that blanketed the country. The incident was simply a reflection of a disease that ails many societies nowadays. It poses a terrible example of what can possibly happen when psychologically and emotionally unstable individuals wreak havoc, regardless of age, social background and country.

Amid the tragedy, a lot of blaming has been done in the effort to assuage the grief that had seemed to blanket the country. Questions have been raised as to whether the killings could have been prevented if the security guard was armed. However, the alarm system that the security guard had used along with the prompt response of the local police did make a significant impact in putting an early end to what could have been another bloody massacre.

According to the official statement issued by the Russian authorities, the incident was an isolated case. However, the authorities consider it as an incident that could help them impose better security measures across the schools in Russia. This is in view of the fact that school killings have grown more rampant across the world.

Columbine High School
Massacre

Columbine High is an idyllic school strategically nestled between the foothills of the Rocky Mountains and the metropolitan area of Denver. A decade ago, the school may have presented the perfect institution to send children to for higher learning.

However, in later years, the school had become a byword for one of the most gruesome school shootings in history. In fact, Columbine High had turned into a worldwide contagion of sorts when it comes to rampages in schools. Without a doubt, the Columbine high school massacre is one of the bloodiest and most disturbing school attacks, even up to this day.

Unrepentant Killers

What makes the Columbine school massacre different from all the other shootings? While the others may have been spurred by anger and hatred, the two perpetrators were seen laughing and howling while performing the horrific act, as if they were having the most enjoyable time of their lives.

In comparison to other school shootings that occurred in United States, which mostly unfolded in remote localities like Kentucky, West Paducah and Arkansas, this one happened in an area that is just 30 minutes away from a major media hub. In fact, the television crews of Denver were able to document the horrors as they unfolded. Suffice it to say, the cameras never stopped rolling for a week as they covered the Columbine High massacre.

The cameras captured the tragic event, which showed one dead body left in the parking lot, the same body that the students had to pass as they ran out of the school building. There was also one victim who was hit badly in the head, legs and arms and was recorded as he struggled to hoist his broken body out of the school. He pirouetted across the window ledge and simply allowed his body to tumble towards two waiting police officers. All these had been broadcasted on live television for all to see.

After the two boys ended their rampage, they decided to turn the weapons on themselves. They were found dead in the library, along with ten of the thirteen students they had murdered.

Harris and Klebold

The perpetrators of the heinous crime that involved 13 murdered victims were two young boys in their senior year at Columbine, Eric Harris and Dylan Klebold. According to accounts of some students, the two sported a Goth-like image similar to Marilyn Manson and called themselves the Trenchcoat Mafia.

Apparently, the group had few friends and often had to endure the derision of the "cool" kids in school. Their small group hated the jocks and were unrepentant racists. It was believed that Harris and Klebold particularly picked April 20, 1999 as it was the birthday of Adolf

Hitler. Based on the investigation, the two supposedly shared resentment against evangelical Christians.

In fact, according to a story that spread after the shooting incident, Cassie Berall, one of the murder victims who was killed in the library, was asked at gunpoint if she happen to believe in God. When she answered yes, Harris snickered and laughed loudly before he pulled the trigger. There were many stories that circulated, some true while others were fabricated, adding fuel to the mass hysteria following the school attack.

The Master Plan

The truth apparently was more sinister. After the incident, an extensive investigation was conducted to determine the motive of the crime. Authorities found out, from Harris' personal website and the private journals of the two boys, that they had in fact planned the massacre for over a year and a half, which was chronicled on the site. The more disturbing discovery was their original plan was to blow up the entire school.

Contrary to what others believed, the killings were not plotted to get anyone in particular. They planned the deed simply because they hated the world and had every intention of enjoying every minute of killing as many people as they possibly could.

In Harris' journal, he had added some disturbing entries that reflected his violent thoughts. He seemed to have a seething anger inside him simmering on the surface, waiting for the boiling point. He wrote graphic descriptions of how he wanted to hurt people, such as breaking arms, ripping off jaws and squishing the heads of his nameless victims. On the other hand, Klebold was depressive and constantly plagued by the idea that he was a failure. This was despite the fact that he belonged to a loving family and enjoyed a privileged background.

Needless to say, the two were quite a pair, each one feeding off the raw and negative emotions of the other.

Homemade Bombs

As it turned out, they had planned meticulously. In the evidence collected by the local police, it was found that they wanted to detonate 2 propane bombs in the school cafeteria, which was supposed to kill over 600 students. The students would have been taking an early lunch on that day, along with the students lounging in the library above it. Once the chaos started with everyone running to the nearest exit, they planned to open fire using semiautomatic weapons from two different positions stationed in the parking area.

It was apparent that they did not hope to survive the rampage. Once they had finished firing at the students, they also had a plan of ramming their cars with propane explosives, directing it in towards the arriving television news teams and rescue workers. They hoped for a death toll of no less than 2,000, which matched the population of their school.

By some stroke of luck, the homemade bombs they had prepared failed to detonate, which forced them to improvise and turned themselves into human machine guns. Harris and Klebold walked around the campus clad in long black coats, which concealed the arsenal tucked beneath it that included pipe bombs, shotguns, knives, semiautomatic pistols and small canister bombs of carbon dioxide.

They started shooting at students as they made their way in and proceeded to spend the next 49 minutes patrolling the cafeteria, hallways and the stairs. However, they also unleashed their firepower in the library. It was said that at one point, the two joked about killing any student wearing a white hat, which prompted one student to hurriedly take off his cap, and he was spared.

Series of Warnings

Prior to the attacks, there was a series of warnings that the authorities had failed to recognize and take action on. First, it was reported that the two boys had threatened their classmates and were said to have been making makeshift pipe bombs. A warrant to search the house of Harris was even applied for, but the search was never performed.

The school also failed to recognize the danger even in view of the fact that Harris had openly spilled his hatred publicly with his online site. In addition, Klebold had also written an essay about a man killing innocent people and enjoying it. While the teacher expressed deep concern upon reading the essay, they apparently bought Klebold's explanation that it was just a fiction story, nothing more.

On the day of the attack, the SWAT team had a series of failures that worsened the situation. This included failing to rescue the PE teacher who eventually bled to death when in fact an early intervention was possible and could have saved the teacher's life.

Today, a number of school killings have used the Columbine shooting as a reference point, as evidence showed similar shootings which occurred in Finland, Germany and Britain as well as in the United States. In fact, the perpetrator of the Virginia Tech massacre in 2007, Seung Hui Cho had referred to Harris and Klebold as 'martyrs.'

On the positive side, the journals and websites that chronicled the thoughts of Harris and Klebold had helped authorities improve the security of the educational facilities. The documents were also used to identify students who could turn out to be potential shooters as well as a contingency plan on how to limit a shooting should one start inside a school.

Santana High School Shooting (2001)

When 15-year-old student Charles Williams stepped inside the bathroom of his school, he claimed that he did not have a concrete plan at the time he started shooting people. Unlike other school shootings that ended with the killers committing suicide, Williams is currently serving 50 years to life in a prison in California.

The Outburst

According to Williams, he committed the act to prove a point to all the kids that bullied him in school. However, he apparently did not have a list of intended targets. He even admitted that some of the students he shot that day were people he liked. According to him, when his finger pulled the trigger, he did not recognize any of them, until it was all too late.

The Santana High School shooting happened in March of 2001, a rampage that lasted approximately 6 minutes and resulted in two deaths of fellow students and 11 wounded along with a teacher and a campus monitor.

It was initially reported that the shootings only happened inside the men's rest room, but according to some witnesses, Williams stepped out into the quad area and then also fired several more rounds. It was told that while opening fire, Williams seemed to be smiling while shooting his gun.

The students were rapidly evacuated to a shopping center in the area where they were instructed to wait for their respective parents to arrive. At the same time, paramedics were dispatched to the scene in order to tend to the injured.

After police officers had surrounded the rest room where Williams has hidden, he finally dropped his .22 caliber revolver, raised both of his hands and declared there was no one else but him responsible for the shootings.

According to students from the same school, Williams was an outcast mainly because he always struggled to fit in. There were friends of Williams who revealed that he had mentioned bringing a gun to school. However, the group did not believe him, as they never took Williams seriously.

The Investigation

Williams had pleaded guilty to the charges, which included two counts of first-degree murder along with 13 counts of attempted murder. One of the dead victims, Brian Zuckor, was said to be a classmate of Williams, whom remembered him in his English class as a nice guy.

After the incident, a series of investigations were conducted in an effort to make sense of the killings. Authorities found that Williams had spent less than a year at Santana High School.

He joined as a freshman student right after he and his father had relocated to the area. They came from a small town in Maryland but the two were forced to move following the divorce of his parents when Williams was just three years old.

Williams stayed with his father while his older brother moved to another state with his mother. To a young, shy and frightened boy, a school with a population of 2,000 students was bigger than the entire town he had lived in back in Maryland.

In Santana, he teamed up with a group of students who smoked marijuana. But despite becoming a part of the "*tough kids*" in school, Williams claims he was bullied. In fact, he was called by many names such as "*faggot*" and "*bitch.*" He felt that he was singled out by the group because he was small and could not put up a decent fight.

In high school, Williams claimed that he was smoking pot almost every day. He shared that it was the only thing that seemed to make him happy; it was his temporary escape from reality. However, he later on shared that the drug had nothing to do with the shooting incident.

The investigation also revealed that Williams had mentioned his interest in guns and the idea of bringing one to school in a conversation with Chris Reynolds, the boyfriend of his mother. Like the others, Reynolds did not take Williams seriously.

In their exchanges, Reynolds even reminded Williams that he did not want a "Columbine" to happen in Santana. Reynolds shared that he remembered Williams' response, reassuring him nothing of that nature would happen and that he was only joking. Williams even said he was not stupid enough to try something like that.

Depression

During the trial, the psychiatrist who was hired by Williams' defense lawyer claimed that the teenager was suffering from depression, which reached the point where he wanted to die. He viewed his life, his present and future as something bleak.

During Christmas break, Williams had the chance to visit his mother and brother, and he practically begged her to allow him to stay. According to the mother, she was reluctant to remove him from the school in the middle of the year and promised her son that he could move in during the summer.

Upon his return to San Diego for the spring semester, Williams found out that his best friend back in Maryland who was suffering from muscular dystrophy passed away. This only fuelled his depression.

In March of the same year, Williams was reprimanded by his favorite teacher in front of the entire class for failing to prepare for their lessons. According to Williams, this was the last straw. He later on divulged that right after class, which was three days before the rampage, he started toying with the idea of bringing a handgun to school.

Life in Prison

After he was sentenced to serve his years in prison, Williams had grown considerably taller, standing 6 foot 3 inches. He was apparently the star student at the school in prison. The prison officials also revealed that Williams was well behaved and had been known to take care of the vulnerable kids.

In an interview, Williams shared that he is deeply sorry for what he had done. In fact, even in court, he revealed that he wanted to tell his victims and their families how sorry he was but could not bring himself to personally apologize.

Williams will only be eligible for parole upon reaching the age of 65, although he personally thinks he will not live long enough to reach that age.

Williams now resides at the Ironwood State Prison, which is a 640-acre facility that houses close to 4,000 inmates. Since his sentencing, there have been several appeals made on the legality of the sentence, given the fact that someone so young was sentenced to spend a lifetime in prison.

There have been a total of six appeals that were filed by supporters of Williams, two of which were filed at the California State Supreme Court and the other four to the Court of Appeals. However, the district court denied his petition back September of 2010. Another appeal is lodged at the 9th circuit; this was according to information provided by the California Attorney General's Office. Williams is classified as a Level Three inmate, which entitles him to an individual cell. This detention requires fenced perimeters as well as armed coverage.

Red Lake Massacre

On March 22, 2005, Red Lake High School, an educational institution located in the northern part of Minnesota, witnessed a gruesome crime that lead to the death of nine people. There were also more than a dozen people wounded from the incident. The Red Lake massacre is considered one of the deadliest shootings at a school since Columbine in 1999.

Random Killing Spree

The person behind the killing spree was a sophomore high school student named Jeffrey James Weise, 16 years old and a descendant of the people of Ojibwe, a Native American origin.

The tragic event took place early Monday afternoon. Weise first shot his grandfather Daryl Lussier, 58 years old, who also happened to be a long time member of the police force in the locality. Along with the old man, he also killed his grandfather's girlfriend who was also in their home at that time.

Weise then wore his grandfather's police issued bulletproof vest, gun belt, took along with him a shotgun and two handguns before driving off to his high school using a police vehicle. He arrived at the school at around three in the afternoon.

On his way in, Weise shot one of the two security guards who were stationed at the entrance of the school. He then started shooting and managed to kill one teacher and five students. Shots were apparently random. According to reports he allegedly asked one student if he believed in God before he wounded the student fatally. Weise then turned the gun on himself and killed himself.

Difficult Life

At first glance, the Red Lake Massacre appeared to be quite similar to previous school shooting incidents. Weise was reportedly a loner and was described as "weird." As a child, he grew up emotionally and physically abused by an alcoholic mother.

It was said that at three months old, his father was able to claim full custody over him. However, for some reason, his mother reclaimed him when he reached three years old. His mother started dating other men. One in particular, Timothy Troy DesJarlait, had also abused him. DesJarlait eventually married Weise's mother and they had two children.

To say James Weise had a troubled childhood is an understatement. In July 1997, his father committed suicide through a fatal shotgun wound to the head. This was after a two-day standoff with the police. Two years later, his mother along with one of her cousins was involved in a major car accident.

Joanne, his mother got out alive but suffered severe brain damage, which forced them to confine her in an institution in Bloomington. With both parents unavailable to take care of him, Weise was placed under the care of his grandmother, along with two paternal aunts.

Because of the traumatic disruption in his family life, Weise had to attend different schools all throughout his early years. In 2001, he had to repeat eighth grade due to issues with truancy and poor academic grades.

When he finally reached middle school, he had to suffer constantly being bullied and taunted by other students who openly made fun of his unusual physical appearance, as well as his preference for wearing all black clothing. Weise was seen by the teachers as a disturbingly "withdrawn" child and was labeled as a "Goth kid." However, he was never seen to have any violent streak although he had a history of troublesome behavior. However, despite these challenges, Weise reportedly had a decent social life and had several friends and even had no problems conversing with girls his age.

Depression

As the months passed, Weise became increasingly depressed with life in general. According to the investigation, the depression was largely due to his personal frustrations with living in Red Lake. For many local kids it was a place where people, in general, chose alcohol over their friends and women were predominantly promiscuous. Red Lake seemed to be a grave that Weise continually made deeper.

Weise had to undergo continuous treatment, which included regular counseling and the intake of the antidepressant medication, Prozac. According to one source, his doctor had increased his dosage just a week before the shooting incident. However, his grandmother countered that Weise had not seen his doctor since February of the same year, although his aunts had expressed concern about the increase in dosage.

Weise was known to have interesting political views. He admired Adolf Hitler, and allegedly posted disturbing revelations about his intention to persuade the other Native Americans in the reservation camp to join the Nazi cause.

At one time, Weise threatened to "shoot up" the school on the day of Hitler's birthday, which also happened to be the 5th year anniversary of the Columbine shooting. This threat had gotten Weise expelled from attending public school and he was forced to simply attend a home schooling program.

One female student said Weise was "anti-social" and was always viewed as the odd one in school. She also claimed the she remembered Weise used to draw pictures that included people wearing small hats that featured the Nazi sign.

The Santana High School massacre is considered the second deadliest school shooting following the Columbine shooting. In the events following the killing spree, Louis Jourdain, the son of the chairman of the band of Chippewa Indians in Red Lake was arrested. Apparently, he was a close friend of Weise and authorities found out that he had a series of incriminating email exchanges with Weise, which were traced online. Jourdain was charged with the conspiracy to commit murder but the charges were eventually dropped when he pleaded guilty.

Understanding the Motive

While it may be impossible to understand the motive behind the killing spree, it was clear that Weise faced quite a difficult personal situation. According to his relatives, Weise was teased a lot and they believed that he eventually "snapped", leading him to open fire at the school he previously went to.

There was one disturbing aspect that Weise shared with other school shooting criminals like the Columbine massacre. Like the other teenage gunmen, Weise had also openly displayed a fascination with racist and fascist ideology.

Suffice it to say, the unexpected incident had badly shaken the residents of the Indian reservation at Red Lake. According to authorities, an estimated 5,000 people lived in the area, nearly all of them were of Indian descents of the Ojibwa tribe, or commonly called the Chippewa. It was also said that 39% of the families on the reservation lived well below the poverty level.

Among the contributing factors of the poverty is the remoteness of the reservation, which does not allow the settlers to reap any decent profit from the casino operation, the major source of revenue for the tribe.

It is safe to say that the school shooting took place in one of the poorest areas of United States. This bleak life and the pervading hopelessness that Weise may have lived with probably contributed to him committing the crime.

Unfortunately, years after the incident, Red Lake seemed to have failed to make a probe on the social implications of the tragic event that took place. They simply treated Weise and the crime he committed as a case of an alienated and highly disturbed teenager. It was clear that they had not taken into consideration the growing dysfunction and blatant brutality that had grown more rampant as the years passed.

Amish School Shooting

October 2, 2006 was supposed to be just any other day of school in Lancaster County, Pennsylvania. It was a usual fall day, where everything seemed peaceful and quiet across the Amish farmlands.

Unusual Occurrence

The serenity was unceremoniously shattered by the deafening sound of gunshots from the inside of the Amish school. By the time the local police arrived at the scene of the crime, the single room schoolhouse was littered with ten dead children ranging from age six to thirteen. All of them had been shot in cold blood by a man named Charles Carl Roberts IV; after the shooting Roberts committed suicide.

While it is true that school shootings had become an increasingly frequent event in the United States, this particular case was unique. For one, compared to other shootings where the perpetrators lived in a far more typical environment, the Amish community was quiet and withdrawn from the rest of society. They had intentionally distanced themselves from the influences of the outside world. In addition, while the killers of other massacres were exposed to violence, the Amish community is known to be the society of gentle people.

The school shooting took place about twelve miles south of the eastern part of Lancaster City, at West Nickel Mines

Amish School. The municipality had inhabitants of about 3,000 people who were Amish and non-Amish.

The school was like any other typical Amish school that featured a single classroom complete with a bell attached to the roof. It also had two rest rooms and a small field along with an enclosed yard. It was said that the structure was built in 1976.

Milk Truck Driver Killer

The class was composed of 26 children ranging from ages 6 to 13, all from different Amish churches in the area. The killer Charles Roberts worked as a dairy truck driver who used to service the entire local Amish community, which included the small farms of a few of his victims.

According to the investigation, nine years earlier, Roberts' wife Amy had given birth to a baby girl, their firstborn. Unfortunately, the baby succumbed to an early death shortly after being born. According to the family, the death of the child greatly affected Roberts. It was said that he never had forgiven God for the death of his child and eventually plotted revenge in a sick, twisted way.

Around 7 o'clock on the day of the incident, Roberts reportedly bade goodbye to his two kids at the bus stop just like any other day. He then drove towards the West Nickel Mines Amish School. Upon walking inside the classroom, some of the students had recognized him. It was also said that on that day, there were four adults who came to visit the class. The small group was composed of the teacher's mother, two sisters-in-law and a sister. One of the women was heavy with child.

As Roberts stepped into the room, the teacher immediately saw the gun he was holding and immediately ask the adults to watch the other children as she ran to call for emergency assistance. A distress call was placed through 911.

It was said that one of the children, a seven-year-old girl named Naomi Rose had started crying and was comforted by the pregnant woman. However, Roberts had demanded that the adults leave the room. He also ordered all the young lads to get out of the room and then instructed the 10 remaining girls to all lay down on the floor with faces toward the blackboard. He then tied both their feet and hands.

Before he killed all the girls, he told them that he was deeply remorseful for what he was about to do but claimed that he was mad at God and he felt the need to castigate the Christian girls as his form of revenge.

When the local police arrived at the scene, Roberts commanded them to evacuate the school premises; otherwise, he would start shooting. He then turned to the girls and told them they will have to pay for the death of his daughter. Thirteen-year-old girl Marian bravely told him to kill her first. This prompted Roberts to start shooting the female students before he committed suicide. When the local police finally broke into the classroom, two of the female students, including the young teenage girl Marian were already dead. The other, Naomi Rose took her last breath while a state trooper was holding her.

Soon after, the emergency staff arrived along with helicopters to transport the wounded girls to the hospital.

Two sisters eventually died by nighttime. Amish parents struggled to grasp reality and simply held on to their belief that the five dead girls were already with Jesus.

Community's Reaction

The news about the Amish shooting incident spread rapidly all throughout the community. It was also featured on the local evening news and was eventually honed in on by national media. Soon, a crowd of photographers, reporters and video teams swarmed into the remote countryside to report the story. While it was always the culture of the Amish village to avoid undue attention and publicity, the event tersely intruded their small, quiet community right in front of the global audience.

Collectively, the Amish community was stricken with grief but it seemed that the horrific crime had greatly affected people far beyond the Amish community. In fact, the day right after the incident, about 1,600 individuals gathered at a local church for a community prayer, while hundreds of other residents met at the other houses of prayer.

After the thick blanket of grief slowly dissipated, some people moved to action. Organizations hosted events and barbeques to raise funds for the victims. There were even 3,000 motorcycle enthusiasts that rode together to form a procession. They were able to raise a staggering $30,000 for one day. The funds that were raised were accepted as donations to the families of each dead Amish girl, and even for the wife and the three young children that Roberts had left behind.

Throughout the weeks that followed, letters, cards and other donations came pouring in from different parts of the world. Most were simply addressed as "Amish Family." Overall, they were able to raise a total of $4 million dollars.

However, while the news focused on the school shooting, the world's attention was riveted by another story, the Amish forgiveness and grace. The Amish community did not point fingers or cast blame. They also refused to hold any press conferences with any lawyers on their side. Instead, they simply reached out with compassion and grace towards the family of the killer and made everyone realize that they too are victims in the sordid incident.

On the afternoon of the school shooting, the grandfather of one of the girls who died openly expressed forgiveness to Charles Roberts. That same day, many of the neighbors of Roberts' family visited their home to comfort them. They invited the family to one of the girl's funeral. In fact, at Charles Roberts' funeral, the Amish mourners far outnumbered the non-Amish ones.

The sad irony of this real life drama is that one man's grief of the untimely death of his daughter drove him to commit a crime because he never could quite forgive God. And yet, when he shot 10 innocent girls in cold blood, the Amish community immediately forgave him and did not hesitate to show compassion towards his family. This is certainly a refreshing change in a world constantly at war, filled with people constantly pointing fingers and playing the blame game.

The Amish culture has always been known to follow the teachings of the Bible. In this particular incident, they were able to live the teachings of forgiveness and show the rest of the world that it is possible to love and forgive unconditionally, as well as place the needs of other people before us, even for those who have slighted us, one way or another.

Sandy Hook Elementary School Shooting

In December of 2012, 20-year old Adam Lanza from Newtown, Connecticut shot and killed twenty children and six staff members. The shooting was considered the most fatal mass shooting in the US and the second deadliest shooting following the Virginia Tech incident.

This controversial mass shooting resulted in a new debate about proper gun control in the US. Proposals were raised like creating an intensive background-check system, or banning the manufacturing or sale of particular types of firearms or magazines that carry more than ten rounds of ammunition.

Background

Newton is situated in Fairfield County, Connecticut and is about ninety kilometers outside of New York City. As of November 2012, the elementary school had just over 450 enrolled children from kindergarten through fourth grade.

On Friday, December 14, Lanza murdered his own mother, Nancy Lanza at their home in Newtown using a small caliber MK II-bolt action rifle. He then drove to Sandy Hook Elementary School. Using his mom's Bushmaster XM15-E2S rifle, he shot his way through the school's glass panels, just next to the locked front entrance of the campus.

The school's senior administrator Dawn Hochsprung and Mary Sherlach, the school psychologist, were having a meeting with members of the faculty when they heard something. Along with Natalie Hammond, a lead teacher, the three went into the school's hall to check where the sound came from until they encountered Lanza. One faculty member said that she heard three women yelling for them to stay put. This then alerted their other colleagues to the potential eminent danger. One math teacher said she also heard Rick Thorne, the school's janitor, yelling for the shooter to put the gun away.

Lanza shot and killed both Sherlach and Hochsprung. Hammond sustained a gunshot wound on her leg and survived after she lay still in the campus' hallway and crawled back to a conference room where she pressed her body securely against the door.

Another nine-year-old student asserted that he heard the shooter say "Put your hands up", and another victim yelling "Don't Shoot!" A number of gunshots were heard over the school's intercom. Some students and teachers took to safety in a closet in the school's gymnasium. The school's therapist, who was also in the faculty meeting with the school principal and psychologist, heard a lot of screaming and then followed by one gunshot after another. Furthermore, a substitute kindergarten teacher was wounded before she was about to close her room's door. A bullet ricocheted, hitting her right in her foot. Although wounded, Lanza did not enter the teacher's classroom.

He then entered the school's main office after killing Sherlach and Hochsprung. Accordingly, he failed to see any people in the room, thus he decided to return to the school's hallway. He made his way to the first-grade classrooms. A substitute teacher, Lauren Rousseau, hid the children in a bathroom. Along with Rachel D'Avino, a behavioral therapist, and Rousseau, both just employed for a week, and fifteen other students from Rousseau's class were killed in the shooting spree. Fourteen of the students were instantly killed on the spot, while one injured student was brought to the hospital but eventually died.

In the investigation, it was found that most of the students and teachers were found crowded in the bathroom. One survivor of the incident, a six-year-old student, was later found alive by police in one of the classrooms. She was hiding in a small nook of the bathroom, and accordingly, she survived after she played dead until everything fell silent. Later on, the child described the killer as an angry man.

After killing all fifteen children, Lanza then proceeded to another first grade classroom. However, there were some conflicting reports as to what transpired from there. Some reports say that Victoria Leigh Soto, the classroom's teacher, had hidden all her students in a bathroom or closet, while other kids hid under their desks. As Soto was approaching the classroom door, Lanza then entered the classroom. When the suspect went into the classroom and saw the children hiding under the desks, he fatally shot all the helpless kids. One of the first graders, Jesse Lewis, yelled at his classmates and told them to run. When Lanza saw what Lewis did, he shot the first-grader.

In another account provided by a surviving kid's dad, it was found that Soto moved the kids to the back of the classroom. Another report from the Hartford Courant said that six kids were able to escape after Lanza's weapon jammed. Kaitlin Roig, a first-grade teacher, hid all her 14 students in one of the bathrooms, barricaded the doors and told them to be quiet in order for them to be safe. Reports show that Lanza bypassed this room after he noticed no presence of kids.

First Response

Around nine in the morning, a 911 call was made which prompted the Newtown 911 to dispatch police following a reported shooting incident at Sandy Hook. The Newton Police Department arrived at the scene four minutes after the 911 was placed, followed by the Connecticut State Police several minutes later.

Both police forces were mobilized with police tactical units, local police dogs, a state police helicopter and a bomb squad. A lock down was raised as police started to evacuate surviving students room by room.

Just after 10 AM, the Danbury Hospital provided extra medical personnel in anticipation of receiving numerous wounded students. Of the three wounded patients taken to the hospital, only one survived, an adult; the two children were declared dead.

On Site Investigation

When an investigation was commenced, police failed to find any messages or suicide notes that would link to the planning of the fatal shootings. Janet Robinson, Newton Schools' Superintendent, said she found no possible connection between the school and the suspect's mother, contrary to initial media reports stating Lanza's mom had worked at the school. Police further investigated reports about the suspect getting involved in an argument with staff members at the school just before the shooting. Based on reports, it was presumed that Lanza first killed the principal and the school psychologist, two of the four school staff that was involved in the argument. He then wounded a third staff member, while one was spared since the staff member was absent from school on that day. However, the state police said they are not aware of the reports about the argument.

It was initially reported that it was Lanza's sibling, Ryan, was the killer because during the time of the incident, the suspect was carrying with him Ryan's identification. Lanza's brother, after getting implicated, submitted himself to the New Jersey State Police, the Federal Bureau of Investigation, and the Connecticut State Police for questioning. Later on, police said they did not consider Ryan Lanza a suspect in the crime and that they negated reports about taking him into custody. Ryan Lanza stated that the last time he kept in touch with Adam was in 2010.

Final Report

On November 25, 2013, a final report was given providing all the reports from the investigation of the shooting. The report concluded that throughout the massacre, Adam Lanza acted alone. It was also noted that Lanza was well familiar with gaining access to ammunition and firearms and that he had an obsession about mass murders. By December of 2013, police finally released pages of documents that pertained to their investigation. To abide by the law, the names of witnesses and victims were withheld. The summary report further included various pieces of information about different items found on the suspect's computer like personal beliefs and writings.

As the authorities closed in on Lanza, he ultimately turned his weapon on himself and committed suicide. This left the community and police little to go on to find answers as to why this tragedy took place.

Rio de Janeiro School Shooting

On the 7th of April in 2011, an armed male went into the Tasso da Silveria Municipal School, a small primary school based in Realengo in the western part of Rio de Janeiro, Brazil. Twelve children, aged between twelve and fourteen were instantly killed, while twelve others were seriously wounded in the first incident of a school shooting in Brazil, which did not involve a gang war that resulted in a huge number of deaths.

The Incident and the Casualties

The lone gunman, identified as Wellington
Oliveira, made his way to the school premises at
8:30 in the morning, local time. He was able to
successfully get on the campus after he
identified himself as an alumnus of the school
and asked for his school record history. Because
he presented himself as he claimed to be, he
easily gained access to the entrance. However,
instead of going to the head office of the school,
he advanced himself to the school's second floor
and entered into an 8th grade classroom. Based
on the accounts of a number of victims, Oliveira
was initially polite to the children. He even
saluted to the students before placing his carrier
bag on the table. However, soon after, he
brutally opened fire on a number of eighth-
graders.

Oliveira came armed with a two handguns: a .32
caliber revolver as well as a .38 caliber revolver
equipped with numbers of speed loaders. One
student who survived in the massacre said that
the perpetrator selectively shot young girls and
shot the boys just to prevent them from
escaping. Of the accounted twelve students
killed, ten of them were girls.

By the time the suspect started shooting, children were running outside the school. As the shooting transpired two police officers in the area were immediately alerted by two of the male students. When the police officers reached the scene, Oliveira had already exited the second-floor classroom and was on his way up to the building's third floor. At this point, teachers and students had already secured themselves by barricading their classrooms. Third Sergeant Marcio Alexandre Alves from the Rio de Janeiro military police then shot the suspect in the stomach and in the leg. Oliveira fell down on the school's staircase. He then pulled the trigger and shot himself in the head, dying instantly.

All the victims were between the ages of twelve and fourteen years old. All except one of the victims were immediately buried a day following the fatal shooting, as required by Brazilian traditions of holding memorial services within a day of the time a person dies. The body of the twelfth victim was then cremated two days after.

The Shooting Suspect

Wellington Menezes Oliveira, born on July 13, 1987, was the twenty-three year old suspect of the Rio de Janeiro school shootings. According to reports, Oliveira was formerly a pupil of Escola Municipal Tasso da Silveria. The local police verified that they had in their custody a letter written by the perpetrator. The letter contained the suspect's intention of committing suicide. Additionally, the local police pointed out that they had failed to find concrete proof of political or religious intentions for the massive attack.

Police found text messages from Oliveira's home that suggested the suspect was much obsessed with terrorist acts. He even described Islam as the most accurate religion. One of the suspect's neighbors was also discovered to have converted to Islam just two years before the attack; he testified that two years prior to the massive attack, Oliveira had already converted to Islam.

Based on his letters, Oliveira said that he had long beforehand attended the local mosque downtown Rio and that he would burn candles for hours a day just to study the Quran. Oliveira described his close association with a certain "Abdul" who was apparently someone from overseas. This "Abdul" even boasted about taking a major part in the September 11 attacks. The twenty-three year-old suspect further stated that he thought about relocating to a country with a Muslim majority, either in Malaysia or in Egypt. Nonetheless, both leaders of Islam and Jehovah's Witness based in Rio de Janeiro denied the suspect's claims.

Background of the Suspect

Oliveira once attended the Tasso da Silveria Municipal School in 1999 until 2002. On the accounts of his former classmates, the suspect was said to be strange and reserved. He was often bullied and harassed constantly by some of his schoolmates and was even called "Sherman", insinuating that of a movie character from the American Pie series. Additionally, he was also called a "suingue" (swing) mainly because of his limping leg. Worse, he was even thrown into a dirty garbage bin.

A couple of days prior to the shooting incident, Oliveira made a video that discussed the bullying and cruelty. He said that the struggles by which a lot of his brothers had lost their lives in the past, and for what he will also die for is not merely because of bullying. Rather, it is also a huge fight against cowards, and cruel people who seamlessly take great advantage of other people's kindness, and prey on the weakness of others who fail to protect themselves.

After the mass shooting, Oliveira's body was not claimed by any of his immediate relatives. Thus, he was laid to rest in a field at Caju Cemetery two weeks after the incident.

The Investigation

According to police investigation, there was an estimate of more than sixty shots fired by the suspect in the mass shooting. Two pistols were found with the suspect's body: a .32 caliber and a .38 caliber revolver, a bandolier with eighteen unused rounds and some speed loaders.

In particular, the .32 caliber snub-nosed Rossi revolver belonged to someone who died back 1994. According to the son of the owner, the revolver was stolen at the time of the death of the owner. Police officers arrested two males who sold the gun illegally to the suspect. However, based on their story, the perpetrator claimed he wanted the revolver for his own protection.

As with the .38 caliber Rossi 971, police officers were still able to trace the original owner of the weapon despite the fact that its original serial number has been removed. The owner was a fifty-seven-year old man who once worked with the suspect in a slaughterhouse from downtown Rio. According to accounts of the suspect, not only did he sell the revolver to Oliveira but also, he sold him a huge amount of ammo and speed loaders. The ammo was presumed to be the same rounds used in the school shooting.

How the Locals Responded

After the fatal mass shooting, Brazil President Dilma Rousseff announced a three-day national mourning. She even shed tears as she gave her speech before the public with regard to the incident. Conversely, Rio de Janeiro Mayor Eduardo Paes and State Governor Sergio Cabral gave their statements at the place of the incident hours after the shooting. Cabral commended the teachers, students and the sergeant that called the policemen. The murder incident had also sparked a nationwide debate on how safe schools in Brazil are. This resulted in the government's drive to implement a disarmament program starting from May 2011 up until the conclusion of the year.

Furthermore, the suspect's house was searched for any incriminating writings, describing Wellington de Oliveira an "Assassino Covarde", a coward murderer. Hundreds of students and residents assembled outside the campus to honor the helpless students who were killed in the shooting. A crowd of protesters had also strategically hung a number of bloodstained flags of Brazil in honor of the mass shooting.

International Response

International press members stated how the incident shocked the Brazilian community knowing that the shooting was the first of its kind that happened in the country. Pope Benedict XVI also showed his remorse over the incident and asked the nation to pray and help put together and nurture a society with lesser violence. Students from the 1999 massacre in Columbine, Colorado made posters to express their thoughts about the tragic shooting incident.

The Rocori High School Shooting

On September 24, 2003, a school shooting incident occurred at the Rocori High School in Cold Spring, Minnesota, USA. John Jason Mclaughlin, a high school freshman, shot and killed another freshman, Seth Bartell, and a seventeen-year-old senior student, Aaron Rollins. Before the shooting happened, the suspect was described as someone who was "quiet and withdrawn", and a student suffering from severe acne.

The Shooting

Armed with a Colt .22 caliber handgun, Mclaughlin arrived at school on September 24, 2003, with the sole intention of shooting Bartell. The suspect claimed that Bartell constantly bullied him over his severe acne. As he went inside the school, he met Rollins and Bartell as the pair was exiting the school's locker room. He immediately shot Bartell in the chest. He fired another shot, but this time it missed Bartell and instead hit the fifteen-year-old Rollins, hitting him in the neck, which killed him instantly.

Bartell tried to flee from the scene, but Mclaughlin followed him and shot him in the forehead. Mark Johnson, the gym coach, confronted the shooter. Initially, Mclaughlin waved his weapon in front of the coach, emptied all the bullets before finally dropping the gun. Coach Johnson then secured the gun before taking Mclaughlin to the school's administration office.

Victim Rollins died on that day, while Bartell was taken to St. Cloud Hospital for treatment of severe brain and head trauma. Sixteen days later, on October 11, 2003, Bartell died.

The Murder Trial

During the murder trial, Mclaughlin claimed that his only intention was to scare and hurt Bartell. The suspect firmly believed that the victim was constantly teasing him, and he had no plans other than shooting him on the shoulder. He further claimed that Rollins was never part of his intended target. Nevertheless, Mclaughlin was found guilty of both first and second-degree murder. He was later sentenced to life in prison in August 2005. At present, Jason McLaughlin is incarcerated at a prison in St. Cloud, Minnesota and is not eligible for parole for more than thirty more years.

The Trial

The Rocori High School shooting trial commenced on July 5, 2005. Mclaughlin's lawyers argued that their client never had any plans of killing anybody; rather, the teen's intention was only to scare the victim Bartell. However, the prosecution disputed, stating that the death of the two students was premeditated, following Mclaughlin's statements to the police that his plans to shoot the victim were contemplated "several days ahead of time". The court brought in six mental health experts to testify in court. Of the six, three experts concurred that Mclaughlin was suffering from schizophrenia, while the other three diagnosed the suspect with an emerging personality disorder and major depression in remission.

The Consecutive Sentences

For the deadly school shooting that happened in Cold Spring in 2003, a judge sentenced Jason Mclaughlin to life in prison. The convicted shooter faces two prison sentences for first and second-degree murder and is not eligible for parole. After the sentencing, the hearing suddenly turned into one emotional affair after testimonies coming both from the victims' families and Jason Mclaughlin's family were heard.

In a full-packed St. Cloud courtroom, the stern Judge Michael Kirk started by asking the suspect Jason Mclaughlin if there is something that he wanted to say before the verdict is given; to which the teenager meekly answered "no".

Before the judge gave his decision, he first told the suspect how the teenager greatly devastated the families of the victims Aaron Rollins and Seth Bartell were. After giving out the verdict, Judge Kirk also reminded the suspect how he had destroyed his own future, and how he had damaged the sense of safety in the community.

With the sentencing done, Rolly Bartell, one of the fathers of the two victims, expressed his stand saying he was pleased with how the judge gave out the verdict, although the fact remains that it will never heal the pain of losing his child. He added that his son will forever be gone and that no amount of time can help turn back the hands of time. Furthermore, Kim Bartell, mother of Seth, said she still finds herself endlessly crying before going to bed at night. Sherri, Aaron Rollin's mother, said she was completely devastated when her son was shot and admitted that the incident has taken a toll on her family. Tom Rollins, the father of Aaron, described his son as someone who has lived his life to the fullest.

Both family members of the slain students asked Judge Kirk to sentence Mclaughlin to the maximum sentence allowed.

On the other hand, the mother of Jason Mclaughlin also testified on the witness stand. She was crying as she tried to read her apologies to the families of the victims. She then went on saying that one of the reasons why the shooting happened was the fact that her son was constantly bullied at Rocori High School. She added that her son was suffering from some sort of a mental illness, and that she believed it would not be effectively treated in prison.

In the criminal trial, Judge Kirk strongly rejected Mclaughlin's mental illness defense. Also, the prosecution claimed that the school shooting happened simply because Mclaughlin was extremely jealous of Seth, and not because the suspect was bullied.

McLaughlin's Video Statement

An hour and a half after the shooting, Jason Mclaughlin gave his statement to investigators. The investigation was recorded and was presented at the murder trial in St. Cloud. At the start of the video, Mclaughlin was sitting alone in a room, looking uncomfortable, and fidgeting every now and then while both his hands were cuffed behind his back. Occasionally, he muttered to himself saying that he was thirsty, while at some point he just put his head down on the table. Ken McDonald, the Minnesota Bureau of Criminal Apprehension agent then showed up in the room and sat across from the teenager. When he asked Mclaughlin if he did in fact shoot the two students, the teenager immediately admitted to committing the crime. The suspect then continued to spill the beans, telling the agent that he was able to smuggle the gun in earlier that morning in a gym bag. When asked what his plans were, Mclaughlin said he intended to shoot some people, adding that he was fed up with being teased and bullied all the time.

He then continued to admit that Seth Bartell, his fellow freshman, constantly picked on him for nearly three years. During the course of the investigation, some students from Rocori High School did confirm that Bartell had teased and bullied Mclaughlin.

The young teenage shooter admitted that he did plan to hurt Bartell for always making fun of his pimples. Mclaughlin insisted that he had no other intention other than to hurt them.

Based on the video alone, the prosecution declared that Mclaughlin already knew what he was about to do that day. And the fact that he shot Bartell right in the head showed that he did not just mean to wound him, but kill him.

However, Mclaughlin's attorney said otherwise. Accordingly, the taped conversation only showed that he did not plan on killing Bartell, let alone kill both students by mistake.
Additionally, Mclaughlin's lawyer planned to raise a mental health defense on the issue, saying that his client's judgment on that fateful day was nothing more than an emerging mental illness that clouded the teenager.

Mclaughlin's father was not spared from the witness stand. The father, David Mclaughlin said he was close to his son and in some instances he had taken the young Mclaughlin to shooting ranges.

As of the present, Jason Mclaughlin is in a state prison in St. Cloud. Judge Kirk stated that the shooter may be transferred to another facility at a later date.

Sparks Middle School Shooting

On October 21, 2013, a young student opened fire at the Sparks Middle School using a handgun he obtained from his parents. When the shooting started students began screaming and the scared students ran for cover. One teacher, who tried to help, was shot dead. Two other students were wounded. This entire tragic event went on for just a few minutes.

As the authorities started their investigation, major details of the incident were still starting to come to light. However, one official described the whole scene at the Sparks Middle School, chaos. Students described how they ran around the school, crying and screaming at the time they heard the gunshots and realized that their safety was at stake. According to reports, the shooter, 12-year-old Jose Reyes, used a handgun he took from his own parents. Sparks Deputy Chief Tom Miller later confirmed that the lone gunman ultimately shot himself using the semi-automatic handgun.

The Victims

Mike Landsberry was a popular and well-loved mathematics teacher at Sparks Middle School. He was shot and killed in the shooting spree as confirmed by Mayor Geno Martini of Sparks. Apart from being a teacher, Mike Landsberry was also a Marine and had served a number of tours of duty in Afghanistan. He was also a Nevada Air International Guard member.

According to Reggie, his brother, Mike was that type of person that could easily drop everything at a whim when you needed some help. He added that his brother earnestly loved teaching and that he loved his students, and he loved coaching them. Families of Landsberry believed that Mike was most probably trying to reach out to the shooter and talk the kid down.

Eyewitness Accounts

Amaya Newton, another student from Sparks Middle School, said she could not believe Reyes could do such a thing. She said that Jose was a nice kid that could easily make you smile especially when you are having a bad day. There were even few times when he volunteered to buy things for the other students just to cheer them up.

Faith Robinson, another student said that she was just standing on one side of the campus buildings when she heard gunshots and saw the math teacher be killed. She said that she was so scared that she ran towards the school and eventually got away from her friends. She admitted that she did start to get worried by the time she tried to give her mom a call. Terra Robinson, her mother, was a stone's throw away from the campus when she received the distressed call of her daughter. When she arrived on the campus, she saw flashes of lights, and panicked parents.

Victim Tried to Convince the Shooter to Put the Gun Down

According to an eyewitness, Thomas Wing, he was walking out of the cafeteria just after having breakfast when surprisingly, he saw a gun. He said that Mike Landsberry was attempting to convince the young gunman to put his weapon down. Then he heard a gunshot, and Thomas ran back to the school's cafeteria before hearing another shot. In the back of his mind, he did not know if he would make it out alive or not.

Emergency Dispatch Calls

The Sparks police department released some of the recorded emergency dispatch calls that indicated the math teacher was fatally shot on the campus playground. One of the two wounded students was hit in the stomach, while the other in the shoulder. Mike Mieras, the Washoe County School District Police Chief said that thankfully, both the students were stable.

Faulty Intercom System

Based on accounts of students and staff members of the school, city officials said that the shooting started at about seven in the morning. One major issue raised was that according to the Sparks Police investigation, the Sparks Middle School's public address system inside the campus was not working when school officials attempted to dispatch Code Red Alerts. Reports show that on the Washoe county school district alone, over twenty intercom systems were expired, and more than thirty were considered expired but still serviceable. According to Chief Operations Officer Pete Etchart, falling into these categories does not necessarily mean that their intercom systems could no longer operate, rather, they were no longer capable of servicing it effectively, and thus it needed to be replaced.

In the case of the Sparks Middle School, Stacy Cooper and Jerry Endres, the principal and vice-principal respectively, tried to issue code red alerts just minutes after the shooting. However, reports show that those announcements were not completely broadcasted on the school's intercom system. Cooper however confirmed that it is common for a public address system to not function properly especially after a long school break.

No Charges Pushed in the Sparks Middle School Shooting

After careful investigation, the local Sparks Police say that they were not pursuing any criminal charges against parents of the seventh-grader Jose Reyes who went on a shooting spree at his school that led to the death of a teacher and wounded two more students.

Days after the tragic October 21 shooting at the Sparks Middle School in Nevada, investigators say that the parents of the 12-year-old gunman Jose Reyes, might be possibly charged if they consciously made the weapon available to young Reyes.

However, as the investigation pushed, Brian Allen, the Sparks Police Chief said that there was no solid proof that the couple did commit a crime. Reports prove that Jose took the handgun from the kitchen cabinet of their home. The child's parents, Jose and Liliana, asserted that they did not have any idea that their child knew they kept a gun there.

The semi-automatic firearm was a Ruger SR9C 9mm, in a silver and black color, and with two magazines; one with a seventeen-round capacity and the other with a ten-round. Although one of these magazines was deemed "high-capacity", neither of the magazines were filled to its full capacity.

The weapon was a gift to the young boy's father by a friend. And since the transaction was private, no National Instant Criminal Background Check System or Brady Check was obliged or completed. Granted, if there was a Brady check, still there were no disqualifying details found during the course of the investigation that would not allow either parent from having their own firearm.

Interviewing the Parents

Investigators conducted both a separate and joint interview of Jose Reyes Mandujano and Liliana Urtiz. Both undeniably said that they never thought their son had any idea of the location of their firearm, let alone had the knowledge to operate one. In fact, their son never showed any passion or interest in firearms and did not have any aggressive behavior. The police were able to prove that the parents did take reasonable steps to securely conceal the firearm within their residence. Overall, the totality of the circumstances and facts did not generally meet the threshold of the NRS 202 300. As such, it did not warrant the charging of both parents for the crime.

However, records show that Jose Reyes-Mandujano, the father of the shooter, was arrested in February 2012 for Child Abuse when he arrived at his son's school and struck the little boy, which caused some injuries. In May of 2012, the older Reyes pled to Misdemeanor Child Abuse.

The investigation failed to pinpoint one solid catalyst for the actions of the young suspect. Evidence indicated that Jose Reyes acted alone and did not communicate his plans with other people. Investigators say that nobody will ever know the intent or motive behind the tragic incident. The suspect did not give signs that he had plans of the shooting. Nonetheless, there were hints and clues that indicated he was in a crisis.

Millard South School Shooting

Located in Omaha, the Millard South High School is a premiere and fully accredited public high school in Nebraska. Established in 1970, the school is a member of the Nebraska School Activities Association.

On the 5th of January in 2011 a senior student from the Millard South high school, Robert Butler Jr., was suspended from the school following an incident where he maneuvered his car to the campus' football field on New Year's Day. Dr. Vicki Kaspar, the school's Assistant Principal was the one who carried out the suspension. After the suspension order was released, Butler Jr. was ushered off the campus by school security.

At around 12:45 PM, young Butler decided to return to school; this time, he carried a .40 caliber Glock pistol that was later found to be owned by his father. He asked to be signed into the Vice Principal's office. By the time he was able to get inside Kaspar's room, he shot the vice principal.

When gunshots were heard, Curtis Chase, Millard South School Principal, immediately ran into the school's hallway. When Butler Jr. saw him, he shot the principal several times in the hips and on the chest. The armed suspect then headed to the front area of the office, randomly firing around. Because of gunshot debris, the school's nurse was not spared from the shooting spree and suffered minor injuries.

Butler then exited the campus, drove for around two miles, and found a parking lot before he shot himself. Later in the investigation, it was found that the suspect had used K2, a certain kind of synthetic cannabis, before the shooting.

Disturbing Facebook Post

Robert Butler Jr., had posted an alarming status update on his Facebook page before the actual shooting happened. His Facebook status message read; "Everybody that used to know me, I'm sorry but Omaha changed me and fucked me up. And the school I attend is even worse. You're gonna hear about the evil shit I did but that fucking school drove me to this. I want you guys to remember me for who I was before this. I greatly affected the lives of the families ruined but I'm sorry. Goodbye."

Who Was Robert Butler, Jr.?

Butler, Jr. was generally new in school. Alex Hayes, Omaha Police Chief, said that Butler was enrolled at Millard South High in November 2010, and was a transferee from Lincoln. He also happened to be a son of a police officer from Omaha.

911 Calls

When the 911 calls were placed from Millard South School, it indicated that about four to five shots were fired from the school's administrative office. Initially, it was reported that both the school's principal and vice principal were wounded.

As the school declared a "Code Red", the campus went on a complete lockdown. Students kept themselves safe in the campus' cafeteria as Butler, Jr. started to open fire. Laura Olson, a junior student from Millard, said that she was about to have her lunch when she saw the principal running towards the cafeteria, and yelling at the students to get in the kitchen quick. The principal was frantically waving his arms as he shouted at the students, and everybody in the cafeteria then knew that this was not a drill, but something serious.

Personal Accounts

John Manna, a resident who lived just two blocks away from Millard South School, could not believe the tragic events. Manna personally knew Vice Principal Kaspar since his son graduated from that same school in 1996.

A sophomore from Millard South School, Jessica Liberator was in the school's cafeteria when the school's administrator rushed inside to inform everyone to secure themselves in the kitchen. She admitted that she began crying when, along with other students, they started to hear someone knocking on the kitchen door.

Butler was a transferee from another school in Lincoln, just about fifty miles southwest of Omaha.

Before the incident happened, Butler posted some rambling Facebook status messages filled with expletives. He was trying to tell everybody about the "evil" things he was about to do and that it was Millard South High School that pushed him to contemplate getting violent. He even wrote that his present situation was worse than that of his previous one, and that his new environment had changed him significantly. However, he was also apologetic about his plans and tried to reach out to people to always remember him for who he truly was. His post ended with a "goodbye".

Conner Gerner, a former classmate of the teenage shooter, confirmed the veracity of the status update. He added that as far as he could remember, Butler, Jr. was an energetic, fun, and outgoing student. In fact, Gerner and Butler, Jr. would sometimes end up getting in trouble for speaking out a lot in class. Nevertheless, despite it all, Gerner believed that Butler, Jr. was relatively a nice person and was far from being a violent student.

Robert Uribe, Robert Butler Jr.'s step grandfather said that when the news broke, everything seemed unreal at first. Apparently, the news did not seem fit with how he knew his polite teen grandson.

As with Butler, Jr.'s former school, officials from Lincoln school refused to give out details about the student records of the teenager. However, Rob Slauson, the principal of the Lincoln Southwest High School, said that Butler Jr. was involved in just a handful of activities before he was transferred to Millard South High School.

Omaha Police Chief Alex Hayes did not provide any details as to the weapon used by the teenage shooter, or how he was able to obtain it. However, because Butler's dad was a present detective of the Omaha Police Department, investigators interviewed the seven-year veteran in hopes that they could learn more about the things that may have led Butler Jr. to the fatal shooting.

Police officers first received the report of the shooting incident at around 12:50 P.M, which led to the total lockdown of the school. However within two hours, students were then released in groups.

As the first batch of students was released, parents started to applaud. There were students who smiled, some raised their hands, while others waves their hands in the air and sported a V for victory sign.

Crysal Losole, a parent and an aunt of two juniors from the school said that she received a frantic phone call from her son during the time when the students were piled up in the kitchen. After seeing and hugging her son later, she admitted that her knees "kinda buckled" after hearing the tragedy.

How it Affected the Neighborhood

The shooting incident at the Millard South School had shaken the entire suburban neighborhood in Omaha. Judy Robison, a local who lived just six houses away from the principal said that while downtown shootings were common, their neighborhood was relatively safe and insulated and that the school shooting had somehow made them more concerned of their safety.

After the incident, students and parents all gathered together for a candlelight vigil. According to one student, "as patriots, we stand together and support each other until the end of time".

Henry Foss High School Shooting

If we were to trace US history, from 1996 to 2006, there had been a total of 80 school shootings that occurred across the country. Among the more recent shootings within school premises happened on January 3, 2007 in Tacoma, Washington. At that time of the year, the staff and students of Henry Foss High School had just returned from their winter vacations. Everyone was in a jovial mood following the holiday break but the festive atmosphere was unceremoniously pierced by the sound of a gunshot that caused panic and alarm.

Senseless Attack

At around 7:25 in the morning, an 18-year-old student Douglas Chanthabouly casually approached another student, 17-year-old Samnang Kok, along the school's hallway of lockers. During this time of the day, all students were preparing for their first period classes.

However, Chanthabouly apparently had no plans of attending his class as he pulled out a gun and brusquely shot Kok right in the head. According to eyewitnesses, Chanthabouly shot at a distance of about one foot. After a second of deafening silence and before other students in the vicinity could react, Chanthabouly pulled the trigger again, this time he fired two more shots targeting the body of Kok.

Amid the chaos brought about by the shooting, Chanthabouly had managed to walk out of the building without any hindrance. School employees hurriedly applied CPR on Kok but it was clear that the victim had already died from fatal gunshot wounds.

Several minutes later, the suspect was apprehended in close proximity of the school where the shooting happened. Initially, Chanthabouly denied that he and Kok knew each other. He also refused to divulge the underlying motive of the killing, claiming he simply refused to tell them and that he did not want the real reason to be broadcasted in the news. It was a clear example of senseless violence that had a jarring impact on the students and the society as a whole. Chanthabouly was charged with first-degree murder.

Motive Unknown

As the victim lay dead and the rest of the students were scrambling for their own safety, Chanthabouly immediately darted towards the double doors. A couple of hours later, Chanthabouly was arrested by the authorities and was immediately booked and investigated on the first-degree murder case.

Kok was of Cambodian descent. Interestingly, his first name Samnang means "fortunate" or "lucky" in their native language. According to Kok's mother, who happened to be pregnant at the time, they migrated to the United States in the hopes of raising her family in freedom.

In the investigation that ensued following the incident, it was found that Kok at a young age was also a father of an 18th month old son named Makhai with his girlfriend, Tiari Johnson. Kok was remembered as someone who was a smart, kind and sweet teenager that certainly did not deserve to die at such a young age.

About six miles from Kok's house, Chanthabouly's own mother was weeping in earnest. The suspect's entire family was in shock. According to his parents, Chanthabouly was not the type to go around hurting people, much less put a bullet through their head. He also did not have any criminal record according to the local police.

However, it was later found that Chanthabouly had a history of mental ailments and was speculated to be suffering from schizophrenia.

Henry Foss High School was locked down after the shooting incident and the classes were cancelled, with all students asked to go straight to their respective homes.

The Trial

Following his arrest, Chanthabouly was interviewed by the local mental health staff. According to the files gathered by the authorities, Chanthabouly had a history of being admitted to a psychiatric facility in Kirkland. This was two years after the teenager had also attempted suicide.

According to the report, Chanthabouly seemed depressed and confused all throughout the interview. On his first night in jail, he was placed under close surveillance. The police officer that arrested Chanthabouly after the shooting said that they found the boy wandering aimlessly around the neighborhood.

The state charged Douglass Chanthabouly with first-degree murder. This was with the allegation that the crime was executed with premeditated intent. However, before the trial was set, Chanthabouly's lawyers had moved to dismiss the charges on the grounds of insanity.

The court ordered a forensic evaluation, which was conducted at Western State Hospital, and it was established that the teenager was competent to stand trial. During pre-trial, Chanthabouly moved for acquittal, claiming insanity. The hearing lasted for three days, wherein five witnesses were called to the stand. This included the four police officers that talked and interviewed Chanthabouly on the same day the crime was committed.

The police officers testified that all throughout his arrest, Chanthabouly had been quiet and cooperative and he was able to respond well to the questions. However, in the later part of the interview, it was noted that Chanthabouly's hands were visibly shaking. According to the police, they were able to establish that the teenager was well aware why he was arrested and held in custody. He also showed full understanding of the nature of the crime he had committed and its repercussions.

When Chanthabouly was asked about the death of Kok, the former did not deny killing the victim. Chanthabouly claimed that the crime did not involve money, girls or an issue of respect. He also divulged that he could not remember how many times he had pulled the trigger.

When he was asked as to why he killed Kok, Chanthabouly simply answered that he did so because it would be in the news. Chanthabouly was able to identify Kok during the interview and claimed that while he knew the guy, he did not personally hang out with Kok. It was also noted that Chanthabouly had asked if he would be given the death penalty but later on added it doesn't really matter as he fully expected to die in prison old and gray, either that or he would get killed inside.

When the interviewers asked Chanthabouly about the gun, he claimed that he usually carried the 9 mm as a form of protection. Observers of the interview claim that Chanthabouly was responsive and exceptionally calm and soft-spoken.

In addition, a doctor was also hired to conduct a thorough forensic evaluation following the order of the court. In order to complete the report, the doctor had to conduct an interview with Chanthabouly on eight separate occasions. All throughout, Chanthabouly remained to give goal-oriented and logical thought processes and was found to be capable of answering questions in a relevant manner.

Doctors who conducted the interviews were able to collect relevant information such as Chanthabouly claiming he was greatly depressed throughout the winter break and that he had heard a lot of voices that were mostly accusatory in nature.

It was later on concluded that Chanthabouly did not meet both the legal and psychiatric definition of insanity. They were able to determine that Chanthabouly was capable of distinguishing the difference between right or wrong at the time of the crime. In addition, Chanthabouly's action of fleeing from the crime scene also demonstrated his "consciousness of guilt" which indicated that he was fully